Life Like Winter Wheat

The Emergence of Wonder, Joy and Praise

Evie Hamlin

Ruth J. Reinertson Peterson

Ruth J Reinertson Peterson
aug 7, 2005

PublishAmerica
Baltimore

First printing

ISBN: 1-4137-3783-8
PUBLISHED BY PUBLISHAMERICA, LLLP
www.publishamerica.com
Baltimore

Printed in the United States of America

To my husband,
Luther E. Peterson

Acknowledgments

With recognition of God's love, patience
and encouragement received through my
husband and editor Luther, and our
children, Maren, Kurt, Mark, Deaune,
Jeff, and Holly, in our growth together
as children of God!

A whole lifetime of thanksgiving can
only begin to express the joy and help
they have provided in this venture!

We thank God also for our patient
computer teaching and technical assisting
neighbor, Fred Olson, my sisters for
providing input, vacation lodging and a quiet
place to write, and many friends who
encouraged me!

Thanks to you all, Ruth J. Reinertson Peterson

Introduction

Ruth Peterson, who has
been a periodic poet across
the years, has gathered her
Christmas poems and other
favorites into this little volume.

Her poems witness to the
human love and divine grace that
sustain our lives and give us joy!

Lowell O.Erdahl
Bishop, Emeritus
Evangelical Lutheran Church
of America
Saint Paul Area Synod

Foreword to poems–please read!

Fr. Michel Quoist in the foreword to his book *Christ Is Alive*, published in 1972 by Doubleday, states, "I wish to write nothing but what has been lived … what I have discovered in the spiritual experience of men of our time. If these two approaches to truth converge and we find ourselves before the same Lord, who today awaits us, then I am wholly satisfied. It is a sign that the Holy Spirit walks with those who faithfully try to know and to live Christ Jesus." Then Quoist calls for "the layman to take up his pen and preach Christ Jesus."

This challenge made me realize that the Christmas poems that I, as a lay person, had written each year, sprang out of experiencing that same God in our lives as we grow in God's love for us and for God's people!

It is my hope that through these writings you may see something of God's presence in everyday living! That amid threats of total destruction and fears of loss of life, children, faith, security, reputation, friends, mobility, or partner, you will know that Christ does quiet all fears!

By calling us to share God's love with each one we meet, God also promises, "I am with you always!" Trusting God's ability to speak and work through each of us, we do experience God's peace in a loving forgiveness and faith that God can handle any mistakes or weaknesses and even use them for good at times!

We begin seeing God working in and through others who may not even know of God's presence, and know again the power of this Presence in the world that we thought was forsaken by

God! Surprised again by Joy and thankful confidence we ask "Lord, I believe, take my unbelief and use me to fulfill Your purpose for my life!

All are God's beloved! All are promised God's help! All are called in every walk of life, in every city or country! Do our perceived needs and desires come first, before others? Before God's call? Do we dare trust our creator, who knows our needs better then we do, to fire in us a passion for bringing each other an experience of God's great love for them also? These are questions God helps us answer daily, as we grow in God's presence.

Ruth J. Reinertson Peterson, '03

Contents

Hosanna!

Why such a shout at Christmas?
Why so glad He has come?
Why not? When He's brought to us
New Life and incomparable Love!!
Hosanna! Hosanna! Hosanna!

"Like telling someone you love
That you really love them,
Ten hundred times not enough!"
May You each know the Joy of that love!
Hosanna! Hosanna! Hosanna!
1966 rjp

God's Might

Would that we were more aware
Of the mercy there is
In this gift we receive,
God's Only Son!

Would that we were more aware
Of the might of our God;
The might of His patience
Waiting for us to see
God in others!

Would that we were more aware
Of gifts of His love,
Fearlessness, joy, patience,
And peace he wants to give
To them through us!

1967 rjp

If God's Hand Be Black

The Hand that blesses,
The Hand that gives,
If It be black
Can we give thanks?

The Hand that points
Toward work to do,
If It be red
Can we follow through?

The Hand that teaches
To humbly walk,
If It has open festering wounds
Need we balk?

The Hand that shares
With us Its wealth
Of Culture, lore and even tact
Can we respect?

Enlighten us Lord Jesus Christ
What e're Thy color, form or class.
Join our hands with Thine in peace
That fear and hate, not love, may cease.
1968 rjp

Greeting

If only we, as God's people and social status,
can wake up to take seriously the
destructiveness of the vast hatred around and in us
and in honest desperation beg for God's power of
love to be put to work in us!
This is our prayer for the new year!

A new light has come to our house
This Epiphany season;

Holly Christine Peterson
Arrived January 7th at the
Bubbling, Sparkling, Life Embracing
Age of 14 months!

God grant that the miracle of God's love
Will enable us to make this world
Worth embracing for all God's children.
1968 rjp

January 1969
Luther and Ruth Peterson, aging
Maren, age 12, Kurt, age 10, Holly, age 1
Mark, age 8, Deaune, age 6, Jeff, age 4

Christmas Now

Christ, where are you
    In the steps I take?
Christ, where are you
    In the place my life is spent?
Christ, are you a part of me?
    Or are you begging freedom's break
From confines deep within, unlent?

Do I hear your call for help?
    Your call to change my path from self?
In me, a purpose to fulfill?
    What is it, Lord? Where is that hill?
Oh Christ, speak loud! Direct my time.
    So short is life, to not express
Your unique gifts with us invest'd.

I hear, Oh Christ. Keep me in tune,
    To feel with You the frustrate lame,
    The cold of shame, the façade of fame.
Give through me, Christ, the freeing love,
    The warmth of "come," the wealth of "care."
Unleash me more from bonds of "judge,"
    Of fear, propriety and store.
Unleash to give, as you do—more!

Oh Christ , where are you, but in the steps we take!
Where are You? If not a part of me?
1969 rjp

Joy to the World!

For us He came! You said it, Lord
    That we may joyful be.
Then why, my God, this weight of guilt,
    This burden for my neighbor felt?
Is sin depriving me of Joy?
    By saying I must be your "Boy?"

This isn't freedom, Lord, for me!
    It's bondage pure and simply!
Where is the Joy you wish for me?
    Is there a clue in this event,
Your being Man from heaven sent?
    What did you mean "Joy to the World?"
Why did you have to be dethroned,
    From infinite to finite hurled?
There's strength beyond our own displayed,
    As angels, dove, and men relay!

Your humanness, yet kin to God!
    His Power in You. Is that it, Lord?
But Him in me? Another fare!
    There's too much "mine" already there.
My wish to be responsible,
    My fear of failure, hate of sloth!
Can these be wrong, Great God of Love?
    Can they keep me from humble awe,
From helplessness that to you calls?

Yet God brought Glory down to naught,
    Can't He change naught to Glory still?
In human form you once abode,
    Can't You without my help control,
And hate and fear and pride unload?
    To recreate new life? Behold!
That's why you came! That's why you're here!
    Joy to the world! I live! I'm free!
To know that you, Great God, Love me!
1970 rjp

Alleluia

He came as a human
    Quite willing to share,
The limits of mortality.
    He lived in the helpless
Dependence of youth,
    The frustration of what could be.

Then into adulthood
    He reached out in love
To tell of His own Father, God.
    And how we can serve Him.
Then died and arose
    To show us that we too will live!

Insignificant birth,
    Omnipotent God!
Such love we cannot understand.
    We can only acclaim
Give Praise to His name,
    And know we are safe in His hand!
                    1971 rjp

My Brother, God.

I stand on top of my mountain, God,
    And pray for the throngs to behold,
And I see not my need
    Nor my brothers, Lord,
For the pleasure of seeing me.

Or I grovel in pity and unjust reports
    And demand that my brother must give.
And I see not my need
    Nor my brother's, Lord
For the hate that is seething within.

Then humbly you came, a man in need,
    A babe dependent and frail.
We saw you ask of your Father God,
    For the strength you didn't have,
When you wept and you hurt
    And you struggled with want
For your brother, your fellow man.

I, too, born a man, frail, dependent on love,
    I, too, confess then my need.
And I see now, my goal
    And my brother, God.
As your Love has set me free.

1972 rjp

God's Gift

This birth, 2000 years ago,
  A gift to you and me?
This gift that ended, too, in death
  Upon a robbers tree!
What do I have my reason for
  To swallow all that tale,
How can another's birth and death
  Cause me, now, not to fail?

Well, maybe Yes – His teachings serve
  To bring out good in some.
May ev'n have had a part in time
  The past from which we've come.
But even that's a bloody mess,
  A contradiction sure.
No motive then, or now, I fear,
  Is ever all ways pure!

Yet you tell me this birth is God.
  Himself a gift to me!
You tell me now He's come to earth
  From guilt to set me free!
Well, guilt, I guess I have a bit,
  With all humanity!
So what's so big! You do your thing!
  And take it on the chin.

You even help your brother out
    A better life to win,
Then this enriches you and yours,
    Why do you talk of sin?
"I am come that you may have life,
    And more abundantly!"
Abundant life; all full of laws,
    And fear of doing "wrong"?

(You've got to be kidding!!)

You're right you know, it's not by laws,
    It's not by critics strong;
That God Himself will free your life
    From guilt and free for song.
It's He himself, He gives to us
    In birth and on the tree.
It's His unfathomable love
    He wants to build in me.

A Love for me just as I am.
    Not what I "soon could be."
A Love that frees me, too, to love
    Unreasonably!
It's He himself that's hurting here
    And needing us around.
It's He Himself in each of you
    That makes this love abound.

Abundant Life, so fully loved
That we can only share!
A Love that takes away all fear
And calls us each to care.
In living thanks and gratitude
We find our freedom won!
And so proclaim all He has done,
You, too, are His loved son!
1973 rjp

Creating Still

Is sin reality today?
   Is 'savior' needed? How?
We've grown beyond those bonds a way.
   Guilt must not shape our 'now'!

Yet separation from our God
   Finds hate and sorrow strong.
It can't be right to live like this!
   Self Satisfaction, Wrong?

Our lives are busy, scheduled full.
   With people all around.
Choices now flooding on our minds
   From all the World abound.

Others alone in midst of crowds
   Hunger in midst of wealth.
Labor now leaves us leisure time,
   Purpose of life on the line.

"I am in others that you see
I love you as you are!
Do unto those, as I to you.
My love, in you I'll be"

You really love me, as I am?
You can create in me?
To bring to all the kind of love
You shared upon that tree?

You Can! You Can! Oh living God!
You Can create in Me!
You're living still, creating free!
Give, Lord, Your gifts through me!
1974 rjp

Tree-mendous Joy

A tree, a symbol,
  Full of life,
Reaching up
  In spite of strife.

A tree, the shelter,
  For the weak
Speaks softly of
  The peace I seek.

Of trust, of strength,
  Of living green,
That promises
  Eternity.

A tree grew both
  The crib and cross,
Through which God bought
  The lives we lost.

So let it speak
  To you this year,
God's Son! New Life!
  Now Free from fear!

1975 rjp

His Presence

The smile of welcome as we come in the door,
The glove picked up from off the floor,
The hand softly patted with real warmth conveyed,
Your love to another, but we look away
Saying,Where are you Lord? Are you really there?
That's Me, My Son, In Persons Who Care!

We see people now, and from ages of old,
Find love for life in what you told.
We see the planned order from death to new birth,
The rain and the warmth of your life giving earth.
And we turn saying, Lord, Are you really there?
That's Me, My Son, My Love to Still Share!

We hear of a child once born in a stall,
Grown to heal and help those who fall,
Displaying a Power, from evil to save,
And we turn saying Lord, Are you really there?
That's Me My Son, Come Your Sins to Bear!
I Care! I Sent My Only Son,
To Show You All, Vict'ry Is Won!

Forgive our blindness to Presence so near,
Let others in Us, see You Really Here!
1976 rjp

State of the Family

Our hist'ry is fun.
And needs to be writ
For all folk like us
Who tend to furgit.

A fam'ly of nine
Columbian son.
Cook, par excellance!
Andreas can teach French,

Mick, a school driver,
Is now on her own,
Enjoying her pets,
But still needs a phone.

Kurt, scholar, singer
Luther College still stands,
He built up a bunk bed
Fell out on his hands.

Mark, sacking groc'ries,
Graduates in June,
Now looks to college
For art, sports and tune.

"Deed," swim and music,
"A plus" Driver's Ed.
But sheered off a stop sign,
Dad's (new) car, not a dent!

Jeff, ever faithful
In football and band,
Early Communion
Keeps teasing “in hand.”

Holly, still a leader,
Is a scholar and fun,
“Sweet, cool, & connected”
Is her own description!

Lute likes team preaching,
Has church out of debt.
Best Dad and Lover
You’ve ever seen yet!

Me, “Mom,” Social worker,
With senior nutrition,
Church outreach, & Bethel,
Could use a beautician.
(or some sleep)

Our Thanks are to Christ,
Who gives purpose and Joy
To all this living,
Plus all Life yet to come!
Share His Joy!!

1977 rjp

God's Word Among Us

As manger scenes bedeck the mantle
    Fires crackle on the hearth,
I can't think why God Almighty
    Came to visit Planet Earth.

His creation, plants and people,
    Stars throughout the universe,
Yet to speak—Himself make known—
    Sent His Word for us to curse?

Was it worth it? Have we heard Him?
    "Love all 'round you I have sown!"

Has He reaped a harvest from us?
    Is there a repentant cry?
Chosen people, then Apostles,
    Early Churchmen, You and I?

Do we carry on the message?
    "God's own Word has set us free!"
Do we carry on the message?
    "God wants us eternally!"

It's a Love song, ringing through us,
    Through each warm and lonely scene,
Even through all pain and sadness,
    "Come, Upon your Savior lean!"
                        1978 rjp

Peace on Earth

(World)

Mid threats and fears
And starving throngs,
Where are the Saints
To right the wrongs?

(Church)

Perfection ours
In Christ renewed.
Celebration!
"Given for you."

(Method)

Now teach us God;
A Thankful heart
Just needs to give
For peace to start.

(Goal)

Then act through us,
O Gracious God,
That peace may be
Where we have trod.
1979 rjp

(Peace on Earth—may it begin with us)

Christmas Peace

Beyond the maze of Christian do's
And apathy around
We pop an asprin to contend
With the frustration blues.

Is this the call? To beat all wrong
And point at those who don't?
Or is there yet another way
To make His love our song.

A quiet bed amidst the throng
Of Herod's mighty strong.
A child's questions of the wise,
'Mid temple sacrifice.

On silent hills, 'mid jeering hosts,
A man, no rank or posts,
From birth, moved, by God's intent
To heal a world so bent.

Can we be simply "ones He sends"
Not know all He intends?
No need to prosper for His name
Nor seek to win acclaim?

To our rushed world He comes again
Our pace to calm with peace,
That knows it's Him who works in us,
His Kingdom to increase.

1980 rjp

Family Grows

Time and events,
Both joyous and sad
For use by God's presence
To make Tidings Glad.

Spring '81
Jose came to stay.
Then call from St.Olaf
Up Minn'ap'lis way.

Summer trip west,
Jose's kin arrived.
With music and friendship,
Hard goodbyes, survived!

Mickie and Joe
In Waterloo stay.
Deaune, U of I'wa
Still farther away.

Holly & Jeff
With Dad & Mother
Move from family & friends
Still have each other.

Marshal U-High
And Jr. High school
Bring challenge & friendships
Jeff football fame, too!

With warm welcomes,
By folks full of fun.
Olaf Church staff & friends
Have all our hearts won.

Northside Churches,
Luth'ran Coalition
Have Ruth at St. Olaf
"Meals at Home" mission.

Winter Letter,
From So. Paraguay
December finds Jeff there,
A guest of Jose.

Home Holiday
Comes Navy son Mark!
Saw Spain, England, Norway
And bit of Denmark.

From Wyoming,
Venison Jerky,
Archeologist Kurt,
Home for some turkey!

Together share
Light through You given.
We pray God will use us
To make His Love Livin'!

1981 rjp

Lord

Lord of the Mountain
And of the Block,
Lord of our Leisure
And of the Clock,

Lord of the Manger
And of the Star,
Lord of the Inn keep
And Wise Men afar,

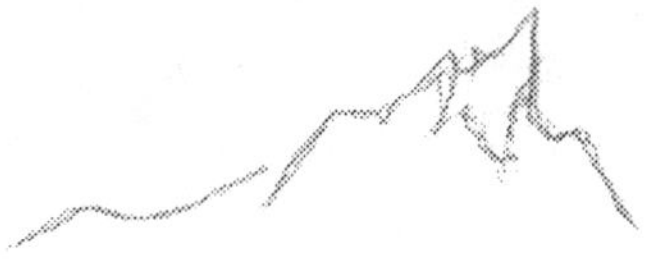

Lord of the Chosen
And of the Thief,
Lord of the Servant
And of the Chief,

Lord of the Atom
And of the Dove,
Lord of all Reason
And of all Love,

Lord of the Rising
And of the Dead,
Lord of the Hungry
And of those Fed,

Lord of This Christmas
And of the Tree,
Lord of Forgiveness
Come Live in Me!
1982 rjp

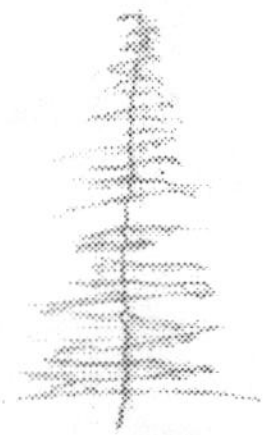

Christmas–Life

From depths of white
    In wintertime
A butterfly
    Flits 'cross my mind,
Then near it's wing
    A sprout, a twig
And Hope appears as Spring.

But what of those
    Whose depths of life
No butterflies
    Of Spring caress?
No freedom wing
    No food, no roots
What hope can they possess?

From warmth of hearth
    In feasting time
A butterfly
    Flits 'cross my mind.
Then on its flight
    A sound, a call
"You still can speak, help us!"

Dear God, not me,
    That's far away
For butterflies?
    Not possibly!
A twig can sprout
    Through depths of white.
Hope springs, if I speak out?

Your Hope in us,
    Your Strength to care,
Your Voice to share!
    Retrain our minds!
Reframe our stance,
    That hope, not death may dance!

He said, "I came
    That they may live
Abundantly!"
    May others see
God here in Our coming
                                        1983 rjp

"And all the ends of the earth
    Shall see the Salvation
Of our God." Isaiah 52:10

The Wreath

I made a wreath this Christmas
    Of weeds and cones and vine
And wrapped it with a ribbon
    And then I called it mine!

The grapevine tough and twisted
    Entwined and reaching out,
Became a perfect circle
    To show what love's about.

The starkness of it speaking
    Of thorns thus once entwined,
To crown the Gift and Giver,
    The fruits from which we've dined.

For the sake of the Lord our God,
I will seek your good!
PS 122:9

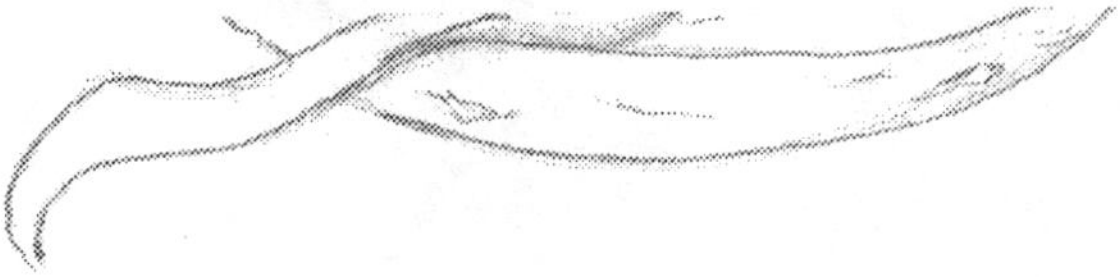

Bedecked with bow and blossom
With olive branch and seed,
The wreath with Dove encircled
Speaks now of more to feed.

I made a wreath this Christmas
With all that I called mine
And wrapped it with a ribbon
And said, "Lord, I am Thine."
1984 rjp

Your Manger

You come to us, oh Loving Lord,
With bedroll on your back,
With hunger scraping raw your wounds
As we take arms and sack!

It's You who's come to us again
In the manger then, and now.
It's You who's hurting here, O Christ.
It's You with the "wrong" frau.

It's you I also see, oh Lord
In "lib'ral" and in "pious"
Each seeking to be wholly yours
With our special bias.

Then to us all your Word entreats,
"Come unto me you ladened!
Take my yoke and learn more of me.
To find rest in your souls."

From you we learn a gentle way,
    Lowly of heart and seeking,
Inviting, feeding, building up,
    Beauty recreating.

Oh living, active, present Lord,
    Use us each as you know best.
Bring healing to these bruised reeds,
    And through us, to the rest.

You have a freedom for us all.
    A Joy for friend and stranger.
When it is You, our source of strength,
    You within the manger!

1985 rjp

Life Like Winter Wheat

When sky & snow blend solid white,
  The shoot of grain awaits new life.
Awaits the warm life-giving flow,
  To feed the hungry from each row!

So sets the Infant in the stall,
  A helpless child so frail, so small.
Entrusted to this earthly care
  To free each one from sin we bear!

These miracles can only be
  Attained by omnipotency
Of one who in creative power
  Has a plan for our every hour.

Open my eyes, Oh God, to see
  Your present plan in life for me.
Growing to trust your completion,
  Even though I don't understand!

Oh Lord, I pray, Thy will be done,
In this Your world, that Peace be won!
Help us to share with those in strife
So all You love may Celebrate Life!
                1986 rjp

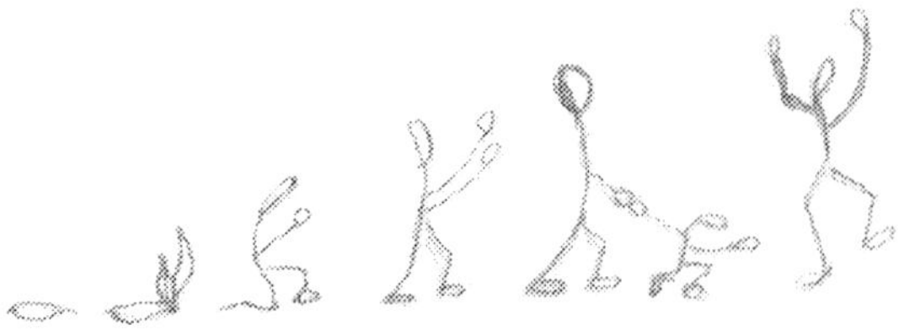

This Family of God
ELCA-1987 merger

Expanding this family
  Through merger and marriage,
We praise God's omnipotent Love!
  Here in Your caring, in
Shared learning and bearing
  In Christ all can see now we're kin.

Will this make a dif'rence
  For Your world to observe?
So many are blinded by self.
  How can we bring love to
The forces of evil?
  Your Spirit where logic is god?

How, God, can you use us
  To tell of your purpose?
To proclaim Your Vict'ry o'er death?
  Your presence as child,
As teacher and servant,
  As sacrifice today as well!

Born in a manger, a
  Low rack used for feeding,
Can we be that manger for you?
  God, that's a big order!
A really big order!
  But, God, You say You can refill.
Lord, fill your whole family,

Each Child of your loving.
Bring life and your Spirit to dwell.
Awake us to hunger,
To loneliness near us.
Your power You promised to all!

Then move us together,
In visible action,
To be your presence in this world.
Calling and gathering,
Eenlighten Your children.
Come Christ through us, Immanuel!
1987 rjp

Advent

Sharing the hearth side
We contemplate peace,
With schedules o'er flowing
Our paths seldom meet.

Why do we worry?
Your love you don't force.
Are we seeking control,
Our right way, not Yours?

The fire's warm crackle,
Flames kindle what's near.
Light dancing and radiant,
Reflecting good cheer!

Flame like God's Spirit
Warm, reaching to friends
In joy, not despairing,
Leaps free, confident!

Come, Holy Spirit
Again in each one!
Breathe this flame now in us!
The Peace of God's Son!
1988 rjp

GOD WITH US

Walls

The Wall destroyed in the East.
   A message of hope resounds!
Could this be God's Act,
   To guide now, our path,
To new ways that peace compounds?

We wide-eyed, watchful people,
   Secure our borders with might.
From child's lost smiles,
   To risk controlled isles,
The walls of our vaults, we site.

"Fear not, I bring you Good News,
   A Savior, who's Christ the Lord!"
The Word become flesh,
   To walk in this mess,
To show this love we can't horde!

What's more, rich in mercy, God
   Still provides, all that we need!
We're not left alone,
   There's power to atone,
God's presence *in* us to heed!

We wide-eyed, watchful people,
   Can we see the Great News here?
We are now all called
   To break out the walled,
And serve this Love without fear!
1989 rjp

Behold! Glad Tidings

In a world of fear
  With faithful few
God acts to bring us
  Salvation new!

Had heavens declare
  To birth God's Son
Protects the Babe from
  King's destruction!

Choosing the lowly
  Of Mary born,
Shows Love in weakness,
  Lives can reform!

Then challenging laws
    He gives His life,
To resurrect all
    From death's cold strife!

Not our works—but God's
    In Spirit's hour
Declare, As Free Gift
    Love's healing Pow'r!

By this God we're chos'n
    Heirs for living.
Authored to Love with
    Great Thanksgiving

1990 rjp

GOD IS HERE

We page through the News each morn.
  Oh, how sad! Oh how bad!
  Who's safe anymore?
Our Hope for the future is torn.
  God is here??

We reach for God's Word in the morn.
  A Woman with Child
  No place to be born,
A Cross! Then New Life warms our dawn!
  GOD IS HERE !

Life stronger than death in God's Son!
A Presence, A Purpose,
The Victory Won!
Our hearts leap with hope, a New Stance!
GOD IS HERE!

The Good News to shout with our voice
Free to share, not demand,
Build up and rejoice,
Calling all to join in the dance!
GOD IS HERE!!
1991 rjp

Family Grown

Can hardly wait to tell you
Of all hap'ning here.
How could we do all,
In just this one year!

Foster care by racist laws!
"Child's color not first,
But sense of self worth"
Holl, State Senate versed!

Moved from EDS Dallas,
Jeff programs for Minn.
Saw Norway with Tor,
Buys home next to kin.

To Aruba, faith sharing
With music and mime,
Mike, De & youth group
Bring Love to our clime.

Mark's long summer of building
Log cabins out West.
Wind blew him inside.
Sees sales job as best!

For Kurt's relig-sci-fiction
A publisher sought.
Works State Port'Entry
New rental house bought.

Mom, "Mickie," works in fact'ry
Dwight Winnebago.
Lute worked their back yard
Corn & tomatoes.

Grandsons Joe, Dave & Kyle
For'st City attend.
As Amy beguiles
Her Daycare and friends.

Suza's Braunschweig family
Opened wide their hearts.
Kirsten's Trivoli,
Bent, Eben in cart.

Norway with Jeff & friend Tor,
And Norsk cousins there
Such warmth & all love.
God gave much to share!

Finding the actual farm
Lute's kin left for sailin'
Lover's path 'cross Mt.
Vigdal to Kilen!

At home we started building
Off kitchen a deck.
Jeff, Mike & friends work.
Uncle Mark inspects!

Ruth ev'dently inspired,
Got knee rebuilt, too.
Tutored by Grandma.
Walks almost like new!

We are full of Thanksgiving
For love shown through you.
We pray that God's presence
Be shared through us, too
1992 rjp

For God So Loved the–What?

God's Creation,
  Sun, Fish, and Plant,
Calls for Mercy!
  We say, "We can't!"

God as Victor
  Son, Flesh and Soul,
With Tasks Bidden
  Offers Control.

Pow'r in Service!
  Life giv'n for me!
Joy in Living
  With Christ in Thee!

This Is Christmas,
  God's Abundance,
To share with great
  Extravagance!

1993 rjp

Read it ! Hear it ! Ask God for the Spirit,
to help us tell of God's Love!

"The desert shall rejoice and blossom …
Strengthen the weak hands
And make firm the feeble knees …
Say to those who are fearful in heart,
Be Strong, Fear not! Behold,
Your God will come and save you!"
Is. 35:1-4

Our kids found these verses
To decorate my room,
Recov'ring again when
My knee needed more Zoom!

How God supplies our needs!
Listen, what do you hear?
Full message of Christmas,
"Have no fear, God is here!

A day full of guests here
    With so many mem'ries
Prepares us for Christmas:
    God was there, God is here!

We had a family.
    God knew how, more than we,
These small hands could erase
    Fear of diversity!

Claim the promise God gives,
    To the fearful we speak.
We, nor neighbors, need fear,
    "God will strengthen the weak!"
                                        1994 rjp

Peace in the Present

Praising God the Creator
Who knows us.

Each day, each way in each other,
As we see,

Acts of love, strength & forgiveness,
All fruits of,

Christ's Vict'ry, in you and in me,
Bringing us,

Eternal life with God's **PEACE**,
Forever!
1995 rjp

So Sing!

Lord, You have seen us through all
    Joys and fears of this year
All family returning home
    Bringing needed support.
Dad's September heart failure,
    Heart transplant awaiting!
Performed daughter's wedding,
    Then hospitalization.

"How shall we sing the Lord's Song?
    In such a foreign land?" (Ps. 137)
Please, Let me put you, oh Lord,
    Above my highest joy!"
Above spouse, vocation, time?
    And again the answer!
"Wait for the Lord, be strong,
    Let your heart take courage! Now!" (Ps. 27:14)

GOD! You do know where we are!!
    "In everything give Thanks,"
Yes! "In the name of the Lord."(Eph. 5)
    With thanks for the medics,
All friends, family and neighbors
    Who prayed God's will be done!
Hope and strength God supplied!
    Each day is God's gift! So Sing!

This is the Great Christmas Word!
 We have the chance to share!
Life with God, here and Always,
 Is ours with Christ's Vict'ry!
With hearts full of Thanksgiving,
 God guiding in Love! So
Sing the Lord's Song with us!
 With Christ in the manger!

1996 rjp

Through the Joys of this year, youngest son's Wedding to Hannah, from Alaska, and Holly's marriage to Koffi from Togo, Africa, their expected child, his Soccer contract here, De and Mike's adopting from Columbia, sons Mark and Kurt moving back to MN, Mickie and Dwight, & grandkids, (Joe, 17, David, Kyle, and Amy) buying home in IA. We continue to see each new day of change as a cherished gift to be used for God's purpose in this world!
With Thanksgiving!

The Heart of Christmas

We've eight new grandchildren,
  Three in this one year,
Six brand new parents with
  Aunts and uncles, interacting,
Each learning to nurture!
  But learning from whom?

"The Word became flesh and
Dwelt among us, full of grace
And truth" John 1:14

God made two new parents,
  Mary and Joseph,
Who trusted God's angels!
  To guide facing dangers and risks,
His birth place, Egypt flight,
  Old saints predictions!

Wise men, Shepherds, Strangers,
  Sent to support them,
Kin, Elizabeth, John,
  Disciples, from strange walks of life,
To share in the telling!
  And Prayer talks with God,

"Lo! I am with you Always"
Matt. 28:20

Who did work in Christ's life,
  Bringing Life from death?
God tells us we have a
  Purpose, Protector, Guide,
For all God created!

1997 rjp

Three One-Year-Olds

So unique in their actions,
   We all delight in the warmth
Of their complete body smiles,
   That spread to each in the room!

They "dance" to the music's beat,
   Eyes op'ning wide at new sounds!
Learning to play with each other
   With pup, toys, water and sand.

So ecstatic in success,
    Such howling at an "owie,"
All exploring in each new place,
    With Faith in their Parents' hands!

Just so close are you, Dear Lord,
    Born to walk the walk with us,
Strength giving, You hold, too, our hands,
    Guide our lives, Cast out our fears!

Hold tight when we "Think We Know."
    Make our Wills at one with Yours!
Teach us the joy in each other
    And how to work out Your plan!

We rejoice in Your promise,
    Psalm 27 we read,
WithThanksgiving and your healing,
May we all fulfill Your Plans!
1998 rjp

VICTORY WON

You, Almighty, Creator, working God,
Came to us on this Your planet
A small baby child,
Man of love and giving,
All to let us know, that You understand!

You let Satan destroy Your human form
Then, Our Lord, You raised it again
Showing Your pow'r o'er death!
God! Can we comprehend
That this victory, You've given to us!

You even forgive our slowness of heart
To accept this gift you have giv'n,
Our greed, our pride and fear,
Then blind complacency
To the power of Your victory won!

Help us also to live, holding Your hand
In this world with evil so strong,
Lifting each one we meet
To see You in themselves
And know that vict'ry You've already won!

1999 rjp

Greeting

Such Great Love that brought God to Earth!
Help us celebrate with Joy and excitement, the
new Life here and hereafter! Grandma R., 94,
a 3 mo. old grandniece, and other close
friends have joined the "cloud of witnesses"
cheering us all on! We thank God for them, for our
renewed health, for 3 new grandbabies this year,
(1 from Columbia again) and for each new day
to share God's love! Lute's visiting homebound
2 day's a week at Central, did Bible studies at
Holden Village and at several churches. We
enjoyed trips to VA, FL, WA, WI, and IA
God Bless each of you, Ruth and Lute.

Gifts of Christmas

My home is your home, God says
And spreads out the morning sun
Across the fields of harvest,
Then sends Christ to host us.

A Babe, Our Mentor, The Son!

So, Lord our home is your home
To cleanse, control, and direct.
No longer mine to give up,
But gifts of yours to share.

As you gave all to us, Lord!

Resurrected Lord of Life,
Raise us from death to give life,
To redistribute your gifts
Meeting your people's needs.

Knowing the peace of your love!

Unconditional Love!
Undeserved pardon!
Hearts full of Thanks!
Freed People
Rejoice
Love
Unconditionally!
2000 rjp

Sending Words

"If you love them, they will know it" *
'Sending Words' that shape our lives.
Words that free us all, from bondage,
I pray, we never forget!

As You came to be one of us,
To feel our pressures and pain;
As You, dear God, though crucified,
Returned to show us Your plan!

You see us each as Your children
And what, in You, we can be,
Free, of **our** limited vision,
From fear of what others see!

"My power I give unto you" *
God's **R**iches **A**t **C**hrist's **E**xpense,
Made "Just-as-if-I'd-never-sinned," *
Sharing with others these gifts!

God! How can we keep so quiet?
Help us to learn how to Sing!
Give us the will to shout Your praise,
The hearts to feel others pain!
2001 rjp

*1—Mom's advice.
*2—Acts 1:8, Romans. 1:16.
*3— Dad's definition of Just-if-i-cation.

Greeting 2001

So many blessings! From the Shenandoah to beautiful eastern Texas, Marshall, MN, Seattle, and Holden Village with family to show the grandkids the deer, and bear, and, of course, the pot shop (clay pots folks!). Then a cruise around the San Jaun Islands in sister Monson's Bayliner named "NOSNOW," which is MONSON upside down. (If we turned over they'd know who we were!) A great family wedding topped off that trip!
*We're thankful for good health, again, great doctors, pastors, family, and friends all praying God's will to be done! Lute really enjoys visitation ministry, hiking, Nordkap male chorus, aerobics, shopping and gardening! (Still a lover of the land.)
* Mick & Dwight in Fertile, Ia. We enjoy the kid's
games, recitals, awards, & gardening their acre.
*Celebrating son Kurt's & Dorrine's wedding!
*Son Mark and Janet planning a June wedding!
Both sons enjoy becoming instant Grandpas!!
You know what that makes us! Step-Greats?
*De & Mike and 2 Colombian sons 4 & 2, getting
acquainted with their new sister, Olivia, hoping to
bring her home from South Am. for Christmas!
*Jeff's (computer prog'r) here, building
addition to their house. He and Hannah and girls
visiting Grandpa Harry & Grandma Siri in Alaska.
*Holly, Koffi & boys in Togo, Africa, meeting
Koffi's mom & family; all are called grandmas and
grandpas there. Not safe in Togo! Home for school
Holl an Educ. Aid & Koffi's night job, soccer coach.
Both back finishing their degrees.
We pray that we all may share the Joy of God's great Love with all those we meet! We thank God for each of you! Please keep God's suffering people in your prayers Ruth & Lute, 2001!

Joy to the World?

Will our children know the Joy?
  Of Giving and forgiving?
Will they know the Joy
  Of thankful hearts that sing?

Will our children know the Joy
  Of Your assuring presence?
Shared even through us
  Who forget You are here?

Will hearts of thanks burst with Joy
  For Your life, given for them?
Forgiveness Complete!
  And Your Spirit to guide!!

Will our children know the Joy,
  Of freedom from judgin' ?
Seeing each they meet
  As God's beloved child?

Will they welcome You with Joy,
  In each one You bring our way?
Reclaiming their worth?
  Your children, called to praise!

Will our children know the Joy
    Doing Your will above all?
Love casting out fear?
    Proclaim Joy to the World!

We join you in giving Thanks
    For our Savior's constant care
Guiding us to share
    This great Good News, not Bad!
                                        2002 rjp

Spirit of God Through Us

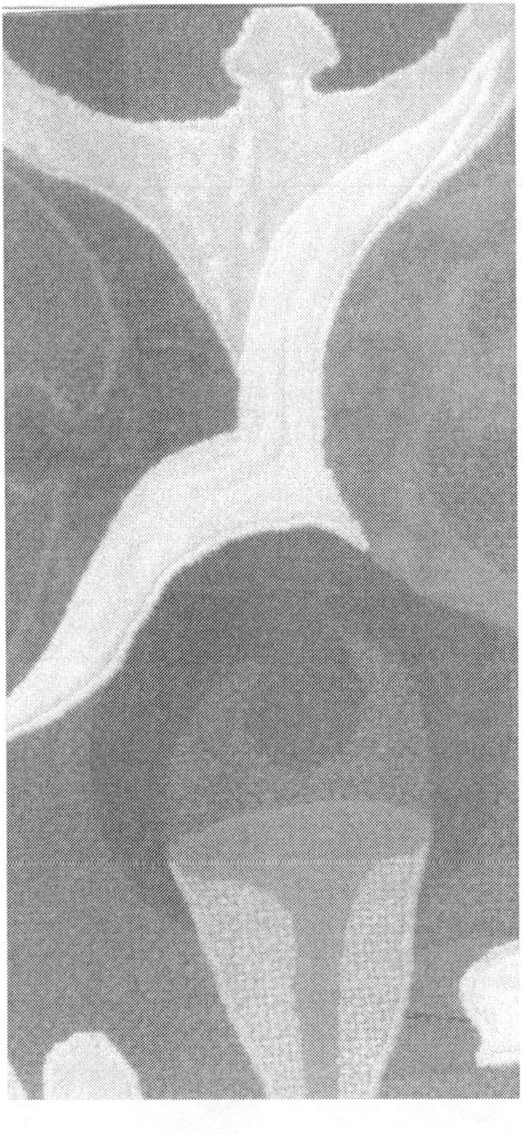

1993 rjp

Walking the Walk

This child of two
Walked abnormally.
Parents prayed, "Lord, help her to walk."
Doctor's help known, brought success!

She walked and she ran
This child of ten,
Encouraged in faith to have fun.
"Lord , she is yours, bring her health."

A limp developed.
More surgical needs.
"Please tell my folks, I'm not afraid,
Jesus is holding my hand."

Parents, so patient
Lifting body casts,
Saw pain that she took for granted,
Through school, marriage, and family.

For the young couple
A challenge to live,
Each day called to God who gives strength
To all who ask for God's help!

New hips discovered
Family encouraged
Prayed," Eight years on crutches enough.
Please, God, may this surgery work!"

"Can you believe it!
Can you believe it !"
Day after, on walker, No pain!!
"Hurt is not part of walking ?? !"

"Lord God, what blessings
You give to this world!
What knowledge you give to our care!
Please, help us find ways to share!"
2003.1 rjp

Alone

In 7th grade we moved
    The city was cold and drab
All alone, I cried to God, " Why?"
    Seems like I heard a sigh!

Sat on the cold back steps
    A squirrel came to watch me pout.
Fin'lly took a nut from my hand.
    A new friend I had found!

"God made you and all life
    And knows and cares for us all,
Sent Jesus to win over death
    Is God's Spirit in us!"

"Yes," I thought, "I believe!"
    "God must be present with me.
We can ask, Why, now and God hears!"
    "Lord, keep me always near!"
                2003.2 rjp

Decisions! Decisions!

Examples of faith
    All around me.
I wanted to do God's will,
    But how do I know
Just what that is?

Yes, I knew, "Be Good!"
    "Love your neighbors!"
But where God wants me to be?
    Who is my neighbor?
Which choice is Good?

One day at a time,
    I kept thinking!
What if I should change my mind?
    To do it my way,
Without God's will?

God's able to keep,
    That which I have
Committed unto God's care.
    Your Word says so, God
Take my Free will!

How will I know what
    You want for me?
"So, Girl, Just what are your plans?"
    "Just not Social Work!
Too much reading!"

Where did I get "A's"?
    In Social Work!
That means to grad. school you go!
    "Lord, I believe, Help!"
"My unbelief!"

Decisions...

This became my prayer.
    Directions came,
Social work child placement
    Tore open my heart!
Can I adopt?

I wanted marriage,
    Love and fam'ly.
"If marriage is not for me,
    Lord , I want your will.
You know Your plan!"

I tell my kids now
    God's plans are Great!
Most exciting life ever!
    Full of surprises,
Grace and support!

Grace is forgiveness,
    Surprising Love,
Christ's life given for us all,
    Defeating death's hold.
Now lives in you!

2003.3 rjp

You Are Wed!

Together in Christ you've a calling!
  Together with all you are His.
Together, to gather God's children
  Together gain strength that God gives!

Together in Christ, with the hurting,
  Together with all, you bring joy.
Together to send out God's children,
  Together share all that God gives.

Together with Christ, new creation.
  Together with all, we have hope.
Together to grow in God's likeness,
  Together, God creates this home.

Then together with God, where ever,
  As we're called, gathered, and grown,
Life finds it's fullest potential, as
  God gathers the seeds that were sown!
                    1983 rjp 2003.4

To Start Each Day

God. You made us
   Now side by side.
You know *Your* plan,
   Our lives to guide!

We start with Thanks
   And then request
That *Your* Purpose
   Will be our quest.

So Thank You Lord
   For this *Your* food,
For Life, and health
   And every good.

May we have Faith,
   And strength this day,
To do *Your* will
   And walk *Your* way.

1955 rjp & lep, as they
began life together! 2003.5

Our First Year

We had just married,
Had small apartment,
When asked to house-sit for Prof.
Professor's health changed our plans!

As grad school began
Two on army cot
Where kind
friends shared living space.
Friends compatible! Cot not!

We beginners learned
Rent traps do exist,
After down payment of rent
No daytime heat nor water!

Friends all were helping,
And housing was found,
Only 'til end of school year!
Time to continue to learn!

Compatible friends
Said, "Shared living worked,"
"Could we help with family,
While husband at training camp?"

Yes, God does provide!
Three months before move
To internship assignment,
A house for us and new child!
2003.6 rjp

Entertaining

Apartment upstairs
   Complete with kitchen.
Brothers with mates come to dinner!
   First family visits, so fun!

The table all set
   All dishes matching
With napkins, and glasses, and chairs.
   Candle, all ready to light.

Big hen from the farm,
   An hour it baked,
Then one and a half pressure cooked!
   No fork, nor knife could dissect!

Did you know they sell
   Cans of pie cherries
So delicious, so beautiful,
   That still contain all their pits?

Did you know brothers
   Don't let you forget?
With grins on everyone's faces,
   The story is oft retold!

2003.7 rjp

Dear Valentine Lute,

I'm so glad I married a Mister
Who spreads Love
with family/home chores.
Though I weaken, despair, or snore
You keep loving me ever more!
And ain't yet
Turned me out to pasture!

You also excel as my Pastor,
My confidant,
Partner, and cook,
Helping tend our kids from the Book.
You gently
Help me to heal faster!

We ask God to keep from disaster,
All those who've
Been giv'n to our care,
With fun, work, The Word, and worship,
We've got all
We could ever ask *fur*!

With great Thanksgiving to God for you,
And for all
That you are to me.
We Celebrate Valentine's Day
In that Love,
You've helped us all to be!
2003.8 rjp

Roses are not always red,
And violets are not always
blue,

But as sure as I love
sharing your bread
(and your bed)
Please know that my love
is all true —
Completely,
always,
intensely
forever!
XOXOXOXOXO

Lute

Nursing Home

A quiet bed,
  A comfort chair,
On which
  My dad relaxed.

His knowing not
  Our family,
We sharing
  News unasked.

Then Mom walked in,
  On nurse aid shift,
Dad's eyes
  Shone bright with Love!

"I want you to
  Meet this lady"
Then reached
  To draw her in!

There must have been
  Some tender care,
That sparks
  That light so strong!

No name, no past,
  Just their shared need!
Brought back
  That glimpse of Dad!

We thank You, Lord
   For Love that strong
That's shared
   So quietly.

Your loving us
   Despite ourselves,
That brings
   A glimpse of You!

2003.9 rjp

Choices

The telephone daily
    Like fire and water
Has power to bless or destroy.
    "God use me to bless!"

A call from a neighbor
    Or tele' marketer,
Each one a child of your making.
    "Use me Lord, to love!"

Caller I.D., It's them.
    They will think I'm not home.
Or do they think, "They know it's us,
    And refuse to hear?"

Are my needs for control
    Greater than their needs, Lord?
Is my time on earth really mine,
    Or a gift to share?

Can I trust You to bring
    Those You want me to meet?
Will You really give me the words?
    Your Word says You will!

Your gifts are so many!
    Lord, teach us their power.
Guide us to use each for Your will,
    Sharing Your presence!
2003.10 rjp

Christian: A Calling

Many hats we're called to wear
  Along the road of life.
Channels of God's Holy Word,
  Of Love and Forgiveness,
Of God's Passion, for us all,
  Gifts, given to our care.

This is no nine to five job!
  A time for myself? Where?
Far away from God's calling?
  Or growing in God's way?
To control my surroundings
  Or trust God to control?

"Why, Lord, when I'm so busy
  Really seeking Your will?
Do You show me other's pain,
  Or tasks beyond my realm?"
"Who disquiets me with fears
  Of inadequacies?"

Cradled in your people's hands,
    You carry us to serve!
In your awesome forgiveness,
    We grow in your great love!
Then we see You in action
    In our everyday lives!

In our friends, in creation,
    Doors that open and don't,
In daily bread from Your Word,
    Your gifts, given through me!
"Please Lord, recreate our lives!
    Teach us Your will to seek!"
                                        2003.11 rjp

Bridge Building

How do we tell you of dreams
   Coming true as we share
The faith of new Leipzig friends
   All due to God's Son!

Begin visit with elders.
   Post war, Germany East,
No Welcome, food or smile,
   Better kind of Feast!

Our German-born Pastor-guide
   Met serious faces.
No "Westerners" yet had dared
   Come to these places!

Asked "How many here have lost
   Sons, husbands, or family?
Then asked of our group the same.
   Both replies equal!

"We don't want this to happen
   Ever again, do we?
Then began humming a hymn
   Known to East and West!

"May we share your books with you?"
As we joined them in song.
Smiles of recognition,
All Children of God!

Visit to Trinitatus
Leipzig Lutheran Church.
What political structure
Will do to Church School.

Pray Church-State Co-op will work,
Who owns our Church and School?
Will youth trust our Christ to Save,
From idol, self rule ?

We recognize this struggle
Is ours as well as theirs.
We join their walk of Faith and
Peace Vigil of prayers.

1992, 2003.12 rjp

Partner, Friend & Lover

How do I know God's love for me?
It's been lived by
The head of our family!
Your dependence on God,
Whose loving and giving,
Flow to all in your care.

How can we Thank God for this gift
Of love through you,
We can try to live like you,
Seeking God at each turn,
Claiming God's promise to
Be in each of us, too!

Hearing that most life will be tough,
That God's Presence
Promised to us is enough!
Not our understanding,
Accolades, giv'n or not,
But Christ's love through our lives!

2003.13, 47th Anniversary rjp

The Question?

Tell me, young generation,
What makes life so full
Or spirits free?
To be surrounded by beauty
Of nature, of hist'ry, of knowledge,
Of arts in sounds, sights and taste?
Many opportunities?

Or to experience the warmth
Of a loving smile?
Being valued?
Each person of whatever state?
Could diff'rences bring understanding?
Or even discord or pain,
Shaping and giving us form?

What of wars, of addictions,
Wasted hours, and lives,
For lack of hope?
What of cruelty beyond thought,
Of destruction, rejection, conceit?
Tell me, Young generation,
The age old question is yours!

Is Evil controlled by Pow'r?
    Or power it's cause?
    Why are we here?
God created or Creator?
    Is decision informed without Faith?
Can we alone right the wrong?
    Or is there a plan for us?

Ask with past generations,
    I believe, Lord, Help
    My unbelief!!
Help us see you in each other,
    God's vict'ry in Christ's resurrection!
Forgiving, loving, guiding,
    Making a difference here!
                1996 rjp

Child at My Door

A young teen at my door, well bundled,
    In ten below zero weather.
"Can I clear your walks?" (All shoveled.)
    "Could I have two dollars, for bus fare?"
Woman watched strolling across the street.
    His mother? "Is she with you?"
"No," he said, looking back,
    As she turned and strolled on.

Child begging for parent's addiction?
    Do I support a habit here?
(Give no money, but meet the need)
They need transportation, south town!
I have so much to get done this week!
"Sorry, hon, I can't do that!"
The words slipped from my lips
As I closed the big door!

God, what am I, to speak of Your Love?
    And still close the door in Your face!
Who am I so weak, yet your child?
    I couldn't drive both of them alone!
Let me not dwell in my shame!
    But beg your forgiveness,
And be awed by your Grace!
2004 rjp

Creator God in Us

Like water and light
    Our sources of life
You are present always,
    Giving us pictures
Of Your own Self!

Water, steam and ice,
    All three are water.
Light, heat, and circling source,
    All three are the sun,
Each three, yet one!

You model your plan
    To relate to us,
Father, Son and Spirit!
    Open our minds that
We reflect—You!

2004 rjp

About the Author

Ruth Junette Peterson is the second of seven children born to Junette Sholl Reinertson and Elmer C. Reinertson, pastor, in Amherst, Wisconsin. The family soon moved to St. Paul, Minnesota, where her father became the pastor of Trinity Lutheran Church. At this time they discovered that Ruth needed to be in a hip cast and braces for two years to correct shallow hip sockets. In 1940 they moved to Forest City, Iowa (Immanuel Lutheran Church), where she led a normal tomboy childhood competing with her two brothers for the attention of their athletic father. Even after two other hip surgeries, her father told her she could become whatever she wanted to be! Her mother advised that "decisions she made for her life were to be made, not as a boy or a girl or as a child of any particular set of parents, but as a beloved child of God who created her for special purposes in this world!"

In 1945, they moved to Minneapolis, Minnesota, where her father became the director of Evangelism of the Norwegian Lutheran Church, and later a District President of the Evangelical Lutheran Church, a forerunner of the present Evangelical Lutheran Church of America.

Ruth graduated from Minnehaha Academy and from St. Olaf College in 1954 with a Lutheran Social Services scholarship for the University of Minnesota School of Social Work and worked in Foster Care Placement.

Ruth married Luther E. Peterson of Viroqua, Wisconsin in 1955. They interned in Chicago at Christ Lutheran Church. After ordination in 1958, Luther served as pastor of Faith

Lutheran Church St. Charles, Minnesota. In 1963 Luther was called to Trinity Lutheran church in St. Paul, later called Hosanna Lutheran.

Ruth and Luther have 3 boys and 3 girls, becoming an interracial family with the 1968 adoption of their third daughter, 14 months old. Luther was called to First Lutheran Church in Waterloo, Iowa, in 1971.

When their youngest entered school, Ruth had both hips replaced. Then she did a quick study of the Federal Older American's Act prior to accepting the position in 1973 as the Area Agency on Aging Director of Congregate Dining under Jay Dahm. They established the first site of 200 seniors daily at the Salvation Army in Waterloo, where Ruth was site manager and set up sites in 4 other counties.

In 1979 she accepted the position of social worker of the Waterloo Salvation Army where she worked until 1981 when Luther was called to St. Olaf Lutheran Church in Minneapolis, Minnesota.

Ruth set up the Meals at Home, North Minneapolis Churches Inc.! Here she completed her Masters degree in Social Work in 1985, with MAH Board members Mary Lou Williams, MSW as Supervisor of Field Placement, and Dick Storla, Director of Northside Social Services, as consultant. Ruth directed Meals at Home for fifteen years with over 350 inspiring volunteers delivering 180 meals per day.

In October 1996 Luther retired one year early due to heart failure. He performed the wedding of their youngest daughter to her Togo-born husband and was put on the Mayo Clinic's heart transplant list in Rochester at month's end. Soon after this, Ruth also retired. With a great outpouring of prayer that God's will would be accomplished, and with excellent medical care, one and a half years later Luther's heart returned to normal without a transplant! Soon after this he became Visitation Pastor at Central Lutheran Church in Minneapolis.

Retirement with expanding family close by has brought exciting opportunities to work in church and community, build relationships, exercise, study, travel, design, and write. So many do not yet know the peace and the surprising opportunities God has for each person on earth!